Stone Upon Stone
In the end, it's a love story.

© 1995 Brian Todd Barnette
© 2011 Peak City Publishing, LLC, and Brian Todd Barnette
© 2016 Bits and Peaces Productions™ and Brian Todd Barnette
© 2018 Bits and Peaces Productions™ and Brian Todd Barnette

written and illustrated by Brian Todd Barnette
published by Bits and Peaces Productions™

Originally published in partnership with Shiloh Burnham and Peak City Publishing in 2011
Thank you for the support.

All rights reserved. No part of this publication may be reproduced, stored in any retrieval system, or transmitted by any means, mechanical, photocopying, recording, digital, or otherwise, without express written permission from the publisher, except by a reviewer who may quote brief passages as part of a review.

Disclaimer: All characters appearing in this work are fictitious. Any resemblance to real persons, living or dead, is purely coincidental.

ISBN- : 978-0-692-07843-3
Library of Congress Control Number: 2018903410

STONE upon STONE
IN THE END, IT'S A LOVE STORY

written and illustrated by   BRIAN TODD BARNETTE

Once, two souls met while walking their paths in life.

And since paths in life are seldom straight or fixed, they decided to walk together for a time. Neither one knew how long their paths would parallel, but it wasn't important for either one to think of the future in a definite, or probable sense.

So together they walked.

They shared quite a bit in their time together.

They found many things to laugh about together and sometimes even cry about together.
It was very good together.

The sun always rose on the same side, and set on the same side.

There were not always flowers, but they learned that flowers come, and flowers go...

and it was best to enjoy the flowers while and when they bloomed.

To be sure, they were to become quite acquainted with one another.

Sometimes they even thought it was best not to talk with one another.

On clear nights in spring they would walk their shared paths, look into the sky and imagine the things that must lay ahead.

Believing in their separate hearts that together they would create these things. and they hoped deep inside their separate souls that the other was believing in the same things.

Once or twice, or perhaps it was slightly more often, there were times when the path was a little too crowded with two complete lives sharing what seemed like such a narrow space.

When this occurred they would step away from each other, each to their own side.

Fortunately life has its own pull and soon they were walking step-in-step, and side-by-side again.

Of course the world could not pull them apart when there was no room to work between them. And they didn't get so far apart that they couldn't reach out and pull the other closer.

It was, by silent and separate admission, the safest they had felt for a while.

On one particularly bright day, one looked down and noticed that somewhere along the walk the other had begun to lay down stones. These stones seemed of no real significance yet their existence was puzzling.

But for a while the stones were basically forgotten, or at least they were not mentioned.

Many flowers and many clear spring nights later,

The first noticed that the stones were still being laid down by the other. Stone upon stone. Just following the journey. Perhaps even marking it in a way.

But now the first could no longer ignore their existence.

The strange thing was, maybe they should still not be talked about. The only thing the first could think to do was to lay down some stones also.

And so it went, stone upon stone.

Then it happened. The stones were openly acknowledged by the pair.

"What are you doing?" asked the second.

"What do you mean what am I doing?" countered the first. "I am only laying down some of these stones, the same as you have been."

"But why are you laying down stones like mine?" asked the second.

"Look," the first defended.
"I need stones also. You shouldn't be the only one who is allowed to lay down stones."

Of course, as happens when two people have begun laying stone upon stone without having discussed why, the issue became the right and privilege to put stone upon stone, not justification or necessity.

That began the real separation. Stone upon stone.

Each had decided that it was in their own best interest to have stones themselves to lay.

So they did.

They were still walking together and sharing many things. But neither one stopped laying the stones.

They didn't mention the stones again, yet, when one thought the other was laying down more, they silently and separately doubled their efforts.

Now as one would expect, they were losing sight of each other and could only see the wall they had helped to create.

Soon enough they were walking different paths.

Remember, paths in life are seldom straight or fixed.

As the days numbered, each thought they could the other somewhere close by. But the effort of laying stones had blurred their vision, and the only certainty was the stone. Stone upon stone.

But the necessity to lay stones by oneself isn't as strong, so soon they each, silently and separately, ceased their efforts.

By this time they were on different paths and again going in different directions.

As time would have it, sometime later in their lives they happened again upon this wall. Which side they were on now would be anyone's guess, for as stated, paths in life are seldom straight or fixed.

As they looked closer, each noticed in the mortar set in the wall, stone upon stone, there was something written.

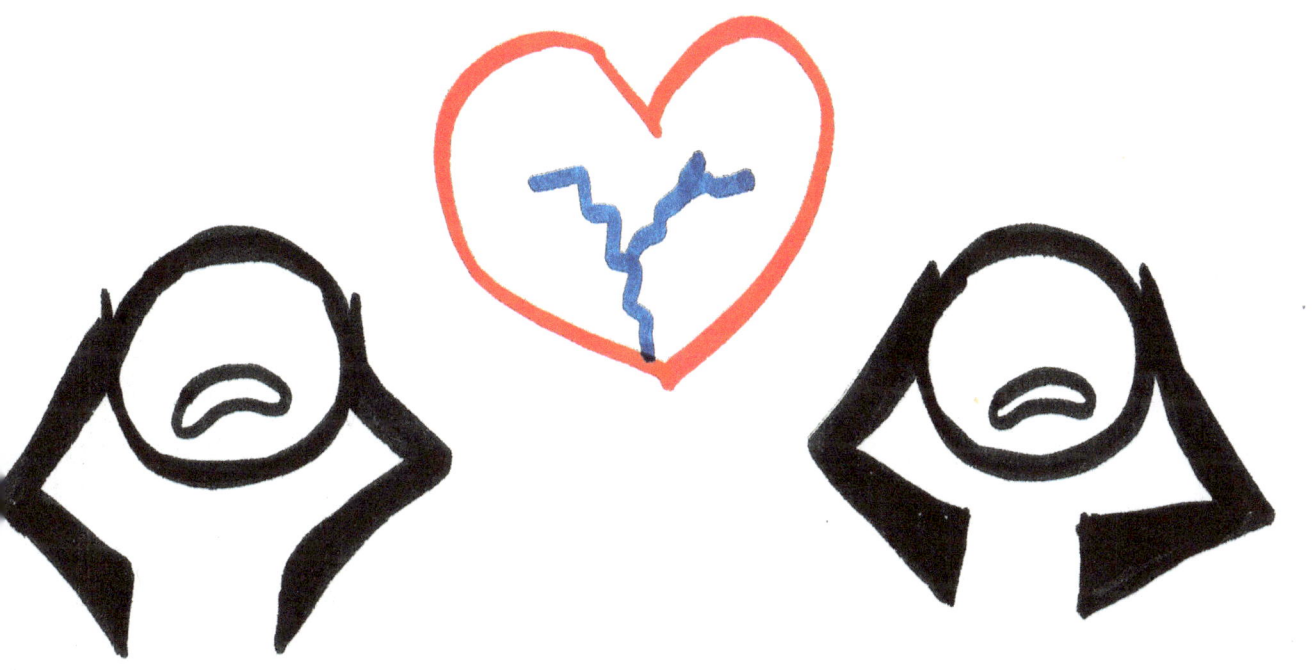

And what they read made them weep as only children know how.

There written between each stone were these words...

Author's note

Sometimes, when a friend reads this story they will say "WAIT! It can't end like that!"

And they are right. It really isn't the end. Its a beginning.

We have all been on each side of such a wall. But it is never too late to recognize this and do what we can to rectify our circumstances. Very often, the undoing of a wall may also be a slow process, stone by stone. But with LOVE and understanding, and yielding to the divinity in ourselves, the wall can simply be obliterated. The "stones" in our own lives can be almost anything that prevents open communication. If we argue, blame, judge, lie, hold resentments or even withhold our own truth so as not to hurt someone else's feelings, we create obstacles to the experience of the relationship. Sometimes its not about being right or wrong, but just realizing that we would do things differently. Also, it doesn't mean that two people are necessarily meant to be in each others lives in any particular way, but it still benefits us to honor ourselves and each other and the time we spent together. This is true of all relationships, between family, romantic partners, friends or coworkers.

DON'T WAIT!

Take a moment and forgive yourself, be gentle and realize that the desire to LOVE and BE LOVED is inherent in us all. Allow people to come back to you with LOVE. And allow yourself enough LOVE to ask forgiveness of others.

May your relationships be paths and bridges, not walls.

Namastè

Dedication page

I just want you to know,

Acknowledgments

This short story has a long list to whom I am very grateful.
God, Spirit, Source, or however you relate
My WHOLE family who may not always understand me
Luna, Dusty, Pepe, Diogi, Toulouse, Cocoa
Sandie Almond for her love and friendship
Maryann Camacho-Chitwood for loving me as family
Patti O'Keefe for "seeing me" and for love and friendship
Flo Rothacker for love, friendship, and a demonstration of faith
Kelly Livingston McCarthy for the wake-up and the immense love
Patricia Nell Warren for her words, and a bit of her time
Tamara Pajic-Lang for friendship and for Paris
Walt Hawkins and Cathy Bennett for friendship and New York
Chad Vierick , and Vince Rango for friendship and Chicago
Judy Goldfarb for friendship and encouragement
Sonja Warg Chestnut for constant love and friendship
Stephanie Shook for the best compliment ever
Anna and Pete Baxley and family, ma famille française
Martha Duell for her example in making a difference
Dean Gilbert, Micky Keel, Amy Bernstein, Laura Lauffer, and more

Thanks to all of the artists that I have been privileged enough to meet and whose work continues to inspire me;
Paige O'Hara and Michael Piontek, Betty Buckley, R.L. Stine, Gregory Siff, Michael Feinstein, Stephen Collins, Faye Grant, Devin Lima, Susan Sarandon, Kim Zimmer, Barbara Lazaroff, Wolfgang Puck, Diane Ladd, Kiki Shepard, Michael Bostick, Ian Schrager, David Barton, Susanne Bartsch, Patti Austin, John Barrowman, Bill Vassar, Michael Macias, and more.

And to SO many friends past and present, who show me constantly who I'd like to be, and to former friends that perhaps showed me who I didn't want to be.

I honor the walk.

About the author;

Brian Todd Barnette was born in Melbourne, Florida. He spent most of his "growing up years" between Florida and North Carolina, attending both UNC-Wilmington, and UCF-Orlando. He graduated with a B.A. in Psychology. Brian enjoys self directed study in motivation and self improvement, inter-personal dynamics, and meta-physics. He has led many discussion groups and has given spiritual consultations to those seeking a better personal understanding of themselves. His interests are in development, enlightenment, and personal growth.

Brian with "RED DOG" by artist Dale Rogers, which Brian donated to the City of Orlando, FL. It stands on the grounds of the Mennello Museum of American Art.

BITS AND PEACES PRODUCTIONS™ IS A MEDIA COMPANY, CREATED BY BRIAN TODD BARNETTE. INFORMATION CAN BE FOUND AT WWW.BITSANDPEACESPRODUCTIONS.COM

www.ingramcontent.com/pod-product-compliance
Lightning Source LLC
Chambersburg PA
CBHW061815290426
44110CB00026B/2877